Bleeding Wounds

Christelle Castelly

BookLeaf
Publishing

India | USA | UK

Presentation by *BookLeaf Publishing*

Web: www.bookleafpub.com

E-mail: info@bookleafpub.com

ISBN: 9789360948801

First edition 2024

ACKNOWLEDGEMENT

Thank You for reading for reading Bleeding Wounds! I appreciate your support and thank you for giving it a chance!

The Abandoned Child Within

Deep inside, I am a child craving attention and affection, but I am constantly being told that I am too old for it.
When the tears run down my cheek I am faced with a finger demanding me to stop that mess, don't be weak.
Deep inside, I am a Child whose heart is shattered, whose world crumbled too soon.
When my mind escapes far, I am pulled right back in when I open my eyes forced to face this reality.
Deep inside, I am a child who's lost and looking for guidance, seeking an identity. Childhood is a time to be imaginative, creative, and joyous, but I was looking to survive.
It was her and I.
I knew where to hide if they came in the house all drowsy, filling the house with high laughter. I learned to push her hair back and dry her sweat as she kneeled over the toilet.
I knew how to tuck her in and warm her some food.
I knew how to run her a bath, scrub her back, and listen to her apologize and cry.

She would rub my cheeks, and I would melt in
her palm as my heart came alive,
Just for my heart to lose it all the next day.
It became a cycle,
one that turned me numb to her tears and her
sorry's.
The toxicity became part of our daily routine.
I became the mother she never was and her the
child who received the care I never had.
She used to seat me in between her legs, braid
my hair with sewing threads, pulling on my
nappy hair while I hissed each time. Those were
the only times I felt her touch. She would touch
my neck to have me turn my head.
she'd massage my hair to get the oils in the
roots,
Those were the good times.
Deep inside, I am a child seeking the love of a
mother and father, but I am constantly being told
I am too old for it.

Canvas

I am homesick for a home I've never known, and
then I realized it was all in my head. All part of a
fantasy, an Ideology fed to me. Blindly
Searching for what I felt I needed but Clueless
about what it was or why I craved it so badly.

Canvas
My body is a canvas,
made from the ashes of hell, torn apart by the
devil to be put back together by him.
My body is a canvas, once glorious and
fabulous.
Carefully drawn upon with a magic wand
two , three strokes of beauty
Until no more.
My body is a canvas,
Covered in red and black from what was once
white and blue.
My body is a canvas,
Carried to the grave to be reborn,
But never into what it once was.

Insecurities

I look nothing like them,
I could never wear what they wear.
beauty to the world is a puzzle I don't fit into.
mines round theirs flat,
theirs small mines wide.
I've tried to fit in that puzzle but turns out,
My insecurities are too large.

The War With Beauty

My self-esteem is as weak as a strand of hair, while my heart is fragile like glass. There's a war between me and the rest of the world that my self-esteem can't fight.

It is the war of beauty.

With a heart as fragile as mine and self-esteem as weak as mine, I was the perfect target, but I fought without the proper armor to protect my heart. I didn't know they would be so harsh. My fingers aren't enough to count the number of times this war brought me to my knees with tears in my eyes. My rivals reminded me why this war was a fight I could never win.

They had astonishing beauty, and I was far from a beauty like theirs. The standards were unreachable yet somehow some managed to reach it. This war had cut me open, drain me of hope and satisfaction. I've bled on the battlefield but there was no rescue team for this one. I found refuge in solitude, hiding in the shadows but I faded away from reality, from myself, and became someone I could not understand. I started a riot with myself, and a dark persona emerged from deep within and demanded chaos. It hunted me, it led me to the edge of the cliff.

Beauty is everything but I am nothing for I am
not a beauty.

I am a broken shell seeking to be made whole by
hands who are indifferent. Seeking to be wanted
by eyes who cannot see and hearts who cannot
love.

I am not enough.

I am not beautiful enough to be fought for. I am
not beautiful enough to be chosen. They don't
look at me. When they do notice, they either
want to fuck or mock, either way, not the best
odds.

Daddy's Princess

She had all the love she could expect while in the womb. Her daddy kneeled and held the mother of his child's belly and spoke to his daughter for the first time.
"I promise you princess, I'll never let anything, or anyone hurt you. My purpose is to care for you, to love you, to protect you, to guide you as my daughter, a piece of me, a piece of the woman I knew would be the best mommy you could ever have".
When time came for his princess to be out in the world, he rushed, stood beside his warrior and held her hand tightly as she pushed out his daughter, the other woman he swore to love besides his wife. He held her in his arms, tears running down his cheeks as she cried.
He rubbed his finger across her chubby cheeks as he stared into her eyes with love and looked at his wife with admiration. But they grow up too fast, something had happened to his precious daughter. Suddenly she had changed, his princess was distant, cold and mysterious.
She always wanted to be alone and responded with short sentences. She seemed disinterested in everything. She always wanted to please

daddy and make him proud which made her pain
harder to bear something he couldn't know
because she was too good at hiding it.
He couldn't protect his daughter from this, how
can he protect his daughter from herself?
Daddy's girl was in a war only she could put an
end to. She knew he couldn't save her, she
looked at him with pain because things changed,
she changed. She avoided her painful reality by
doing what young girls did, drink and smoke till
their brains forget.
But how long till the alcohol wears off and those
shadows became loud again and hover her? Not
too long because the cycle starts again to silence
them. The shadows became her closest friends,
nightmares she couldn't speak of because what
if daddy doesn't believe there were monsters
under the bed, shadowy figures in the closet and
how they breathe loudly, and their nails
scratched the walls keeping her up.
The memories of being infatuated at 16 with one
who knew nothing about love but instead was an
enraged soul and used her as the punching bag.
He took what he could from her, her innocence,
her tenderness, her kindness and her light that
now flickered ready to die out. She kept that
romance a secret which led to sneak outs, sneak
ins and regrets. She blamed herself for her
naivety and her need to feel loved by another

who promised he could. She carried her bruises under her sleeves, under her bra, under her panties and pants.

Her eyes were dull, and her heart lost its rhythm. Her hair would fall as she ran her fingers through them. She was dying inside, and her body was catching up.

In those times he goes and takes a trip down memory lane and remembers his daughter jumping into his arms after work and helping him with his suitcase. She would take off his shoes and make sure he was comfortable. He remembered pushing her on the swing while she laughed and smiled like it was the happiest day of her life.

He remembered when she would hug him, those rarely happened now. He thought of the times he would rush into her bedroom when she'd scream in her sleep because of nightmares. She no longer screamed, she was silent, and daddy stopped rushing in. He remembered when they talked about silly things, they rarely spoke now. He remembered when she would sleep by his side.

What had happened?

Could daddy believe that his princess was no longer a ray of sunshine but a ticking time bomb that could explode at any time? Could he handle that he was unable to protect his daughter when

he founds her in a tub submerged? Could he
handle that he was unable to love his daughter
hard enough when he founds her with her wrists
cut bleeding on the bathroom floor? Could he
handle that he couldn't fight that battle for her
and watched her fade away before his eyes?
A father's worst nightmare is to lose their child
sooner than they should have. He was going to
come face to face with his worst nightmare
when he found his innocent princess on her
bedroom floor unconscious both wrists cut with
the carpet covered in his daughter's blood. He
was shocked, confused and frozen in place.
After a minute it caught up to him and he called
911 hesitating when he said,
"I think my daughter"
He paused.
"I think my daughter was trying to"
He paused,
"To kill herself."
He kneeled beside her, eyes heavy with tears,
and heart heavy with pain and guilt. She was
rushed to the hospital but all he could think
about was why. Why would she want to kill
herself?
Why couldn't she talk to me?
Why did I not see this?
Why after why after why's but he couldn't reach
a conclusion. Mom was back home cleaning up

her baby's blood off the carpet while she cried.
Frustrated with the intense scrubbing, she
screamed at the top of her lungs while the pain
took over her. In the hospital after a couple of
days he went into his daughter's room and sat
beside her on the bed. He looked in her
daughter's eyes was and thought
I am sorry I couldn't protect you from this.
but it wasn't his fault.
"You know I love you more than anything in this
world, you're my daughter."
He said, caressing his daughter's cheek but tears
found their way and she began to tear up and he
held her close and tightly.
"I am so sorry dad, I just felt so dirty, so
unworthy."
She said in between tears.
He didn't ask why right away but after long
hours of cuddling, she opened up and told her
father about the men who took it all from her
when she was 16, she was 19 now and her father
couldn't believe that she kept that relationship
secret while she was abused and taken advantage
of. It started with anger, frustrated that all of this
happened while he was there, he looked at her
and believed her when she'd say,
"I am okay."
when she'd say,
"Hanging out with the girls tonight"

every other night, those were lies, weren't they?
Daddy's princess had changed, and he couldn't
believe it, he couldn't believe that those horrors
happened to his princess, and he couldn't stop it.
She was admitted into a mental hospital and
started therapy. He visited her often, he tried his
best to let go of his anger and be there for his
daughter, protect her, love her, care for her and
guide her.
"I love you sweetheart, and I hope you know
that I'll never stop. I wish you had come to me, I
wish you told me but I will support you through
your recovery and we'll go to Paris like you
always wanted when you were little"
He explained holding on to her hand and she
smiled while tears ran down her eyes…again.
She didn't have to be afraid; she didn't have to
carry it all alone like she convinced herself she
had to.
I love you too.

Silent

I struggle to find the perfect words to explain the
chaos happening within.
I need to keep it all in or I won't win.
My tears have become blood, I need to wipe
them dry and fill in the missing pieces.
It's easy to tell me,
"Just be happy."
But may I remind you, I haven't been happy for
awhile.
It's easy to tell me,
"It'll pass".
But may I remind you, it doesn't feel that way.
It's the opposite, the pain pulls and pulls at my
heart, the tears aren't enough and the cuts aren't
enough.
When I wake, I sigh… there goes the pain
already tugging at my chest.
They mistake my silence for personality but
truly it's the fear to speak, fear to say the wrong
thing and the fear of shame and embarrassment.
I wish for it to let me go, to stop but I find
myself searching for alternatives.
Please, anything to not feel this pain.
It comes for war when the sun goes down, it
torments me.

It's so cold, so lonely.
I want to scream for help,
but I've lost my voice.

Nightmares

I was in a dark place, there was water beneath my feet and nobody in sight but soft whimpers and moans. I followed the sound, and it led me to face a human-sized glass box. Inside was a girl kneeling with her face buried in between her thighs. Her clothes were torn, and her body had bruises and cuts. It was her making these sounds. I approached her and rested my hands on the glass.
"Are you alright?"
I asked her but she kept whimpering and moaning like she was in unbearable pain. She didn't say anything, but her cries were louder. She started to scratch herself with her nails, begging me to let her go. There was nothing but water around us in this dark hole, no exit.
"I don't know how to let you go"
I replied. Then, at an unbelievable speed, she rushed to the glass causing me to lose my balance and I fell into a vast darkness below me. I was in a field of flowers, the sun was bright, the air here was different, and it was clean, fresh, and light. Peaceful.
The clouds were bigger, I could barely see the blue. I could hear the ocean at a distance.

With a wide smile, I ran through the field following the peaceful sound. I pushed through until I could see it. I was alone. I stepped on the sand with another smile I could feel throughout my body and on my cheeks. I closed my eyes and took a deep breath, then jumped in the water with my yellow dress on, swimming like a mermaid. I swam deeper, it became harder to breathe but I didn't want to stop. I wanted to see the hidden gems buried deep. Then I saw this black smoke, it surrounded me. I tried to swim back up, but something pulled on my leg. I looked down and she was pulling me down with her bruised hands, and bloody arms, screaming for me to come with her, so I could let her go. Let her go from what? I could feel a grip on my throat and a hand on my mouth. I screamed but no sounds were coming out. I was afraid, the air around me became thick, and it was suffocating. "You can't get rid of me; you can't run from me, I OWN you."
It said in my ears, I tried to free myself from that girl's grip around my ankle. I kept screaming, crying, and reaching but they pulled me deeper into the vast darkness beneath me.

Mirror on the Wall who's the Saddest of them All?

She has the same face as me and the same eyes but we carry different secrets behind them. The one looking back at me seems desperate to find her way back, she is locked away, abused, and afraid. The one looking back at me has a slow heartbeat, one that could stop at any second. Her voice is a soft whimper, she murmurs her pain into my ears on occasion but I twist her arm and shove her back into her cage because I despise her weakness, I despise her tears, I despise her suffering.

Through my cage beyond this mirror, I can feel the insincere smiles, her laugh the loudest in the crowd, her jokes the funniest in her group. In times alone, she stares at me behind her eyes and I reach out but again she shoves me back into my cage, smiling because everything is fine.

I am not weak, I am not in pain, I don't cry. I am a strong woman, I can endure it all alone, I can make it without facing her and peeling off the secrets behind our eyes.

I am fine.

She told herself but when she'd look in the mirror, she'd look deep to see the thing she

hated the most…pain, she couldn't escape the
loneliness that rested on her chest, the cold as
she slept alone on her bed.
She told herself she was fine, but her mind
played these memories reminding her how not
fine she was.

Thalassophile

I like the beach
I like the sound of the Ocean,
I like to feel the water over my toes,
it tickles.
I like the soft feel of the sand
I can't swim but it won't stop me from going
there as much as I can
take deep breaths
feel the wind on my skin
it gives me goosebumps
makes me feel all warm Inside.
I like the beach
I like to watch people walk by
couples
I wonder how long they've been together
How they met
Does it feel like in the movies or better?
Families, children
I wonder what makes them happy?
What does this moment mean to them?
I can hear people's laugh from where I am,
I can't help but imagine myself with a family,
my husband, and my children walking on the
beach
sharing stories

laughing and feeling warm inside.
I pick some sand
feel the heat from it
it's real
this is real
I am real.
I look back at the ocean
and loneliness came over me
but I push it away
it's okay to be here alone on the beach
I'll find someone
I just need to wait,
I just need to wait.
I smile to myself and repeat the words
"I am fine here"
I take another breath
My body calm
"I am fine here"
I get off the sand
continue my walk on the beach
I smile when the water reaches my feet
It's nice
this is nice
It is real
it is good
I start to run
the cool wind blows against me
the ocean sings to me
the waves come to greet me

I don't know how to swim
but I go Into the water just enough to feel the
ocean
have it close to me
on me.
I am from nature and will go back to it when all
is over, we'll become one again.
Not so lonely when nature is always there to
keep me company.

Battle Scars

I have a piece of broken glass wrapped in a
paper towel sitting on my dresser.
They all walked in and out of my bedroom,
none of them noticed the broken glass I've kept.
When the lights are off,
The house quiet,
That's when I am awake, fighting with my
demons,
Shaking with anxiety,
Talking to myself like a maniac.
I fight but my skin aches for this
I give them what they want,
Blood.
But it's never enough.
Drawn on my skin are the stories of my dark
times.
Times when I wished for no tomorrow because I
predicted it would be as awful as the last.
Dark times when memories of my past kept me
up all night
And hunted me all-day.
Drawn on my skin is a map of the times I
considered overdosing on pills
Days I sat on my bedroom floor sobbing because
I felt my existence was a mistake.

Each time I bled, my mind went silent, but it didn't last long.
Hiding pieces of glass in my drawers
pinching
Biting
Itching till my skin peels
Those were the ways I coped with these feelings of unworthiness, loneliness, and hopelessness.
I felt lost, unable to find my place and connect with people.
I felt different,
I sought love in shady places.
Drawn on my skin are the stories of my dark times,
The times I survived.

Fallen Angel

The Times when life feels hopeless and I've been left alone in a world I can't move through, that's when the devil creeps in to be my friend.
He smiles with eyes that shout danger, he knows I am alone.
He knows I'll never notice his horns.
I am in so much need to feel loved.
I am desperate.
I am in so much need to feel alive.
He pulls me in and dances with me like they never could.
He moves his body against mine and holds me tight.
He whispers in my ears how we're going to take over this world and how our love is unbreakable, infinite, and pure.
He knows my pain and knows there's chaos hidden deep within.
He kisses my neck and bites.
Before I knew it, my twisted horns grew from my scalp.
My eyes were red filled with fury,
My heart filled with darkness and my head clouded with vile thoughts.
I became the devil he wanted me to be while I swam in a pool of sorrow.

The Lies Told to Her

She was told for her to feel empowered she had
to strip naked before men who were too weak to
say no, too lonely to look the other way, and too
arrogant to disappoint. She was told that a
women's power comes from their sexuality, and
she should not be shamed for doing something
men do all the time.
She was told to abort the consequences of her
actions no matter how many times she does the
act, because she's not ready to be a mother.
She was told for her to be free she has to be in
control and have men submit to her.
She was told to only hustle and it's best to never
have children, never marry because they ruin
lives, they hold you back.
She was told to get to the top, even if she has to
sell parts of herself that are sacred, even if she
has to lie and become a slave.
They fed on her desperation,
her loneliness, her confusion, her trauma.
They told her a man caused you pain because all
men cause pain, therefore she should fight to
dominate them cause truthfully, they are
purposeless.

She believed each of their lies. She did as she
was told and slowly began to realize the lies, she
was spoon-fed by people who claimed to be
feminine and people who claimed all they do is
support one another.
She realized the lies when she lived in a big
mansion with a man who knew nothing about
romance, love and sex became the only intimacy
they shared.
She wanted and needed more.
A motherly desire rose, and She had a new
vision.
A life with a child.
But she could only hope it was not too late.
Truth is
Freedom does not come from counting bodies,
but it comes from being a Godly Women.
Empowerment does not come from control,
manipulation or lies, empowerment comes from
doing the will of God.
She realized that truthfully, they were the ones
enslaved all along. Shoving moral values in the
trash all in favor of money and likes. Lifting
butts and Implanting breasts,
all in favor of money and likes.
I love myself
they say but they hate themselves so much they
try everything to alter it until they become
something they can't recognize.

Pain, regret, guilt, and shame live within them,
and to her, that was far from
Freedom

Burn

I stood naked before him, revealing my scars,
my true form free before him.
He stared carefully at my body, his eyes
wandered from my shoulder, down to my breast,
down to my stomach, and up again to my face.
He approached me with a frown, his lips
downward, was it a worry?
Could he truly care about me?
Was he willing to love me and my imperfect
body?
He lifted his hand and touched my shoulder.
I hoped for his touch to be a comfort, but his
touch made my skin burn, it stung like a
thousand knives stabbing me at once.
Should it feel like that?
I resisted that touch, thinking it won't happen
again, but he touched my stomach, and it felt no
different from the first time.
It's just his way of loving me, it must be, right?
He says he loves me, but my body is burning at
his touch.
I resisted, thinking it won't happen again but at
this point, my eyes were filled with tears. He
was torturing me.

And then he touched the most sensitive part of
all, in between my breast.
That's where I held it all in, it was exposed he
could see it now, my love, my desires, my
dreams all exposed to him in between my
breasts.
That's what I thought hell Would feel like.
My body had burn marks from where he touched
before.
In between my breasts Were Red-Hot.
I gasped for air while he stood there watching it
all happen. It was as though he didn't notice the
pain, he was putting me through,
"Please Stop"
His hand dug Deeper into my chest, or he simply
did not care.
He says he loves me, but he breaks me piece by
piece.
"Please"
He kept digging,
Digging for what?
My soul?
He pulled his hands away and I collapsed to the
ground.
How could I have known he would be the one to
burn me so deep?
Could love be so hot that it kills, that it burns,
that it makes you question is it true, is it real?

Such a Fool

She was beautifully tempting and
for any man, beauty was a weakness.
She had innocent features, quiet and reserved.
He was much older and experienced.
She was forbidden to him.
But he was known to be arrogant.
Her youth and innocence drove him to desire her
like she was the rarest kind.
She met him in a time of weakness, a time of
unbearable loneliness, a time of desperation. She
has been deprived of touch, deprived of an
intimacy she craved.
She desired it like one desire oxygen to survive.
She needed to feel close and connected to
someone.
So, a fiery passion grew between them.
A world of pleasure opened its doors. She was
hesitant at first, afraid of the unknown.
Afraid to set free needs she suppressed for very
long.
Knowing God, she knew acting upon these
feelings were wrong in his eyes.
But she made the choice to walk in, ignoring the
murmurs of her heart, the ones that warned her.
She was ready to be someone different.

She was ready to be desired.
So, like a fool she allowed his lips to travel up
her neck, then down to her breast.
She allowed his lips to taste her sweetness.
Like a fool, she called his name, and it hasn't
left her mind since.
Her heart was weak, her mind was weak.
And so was her self-esteem, despite the beauty
and intelligence she held.
Her will to please had him at an advantage, all
he had to say was "please" and she pleased and
with a foolish heart believed he was good.
She offered herself and dropped the protective
veil around her heart, but her soul was tied to the
wrong man.

My Heart's Truth

Mommy said she was as beautiful as the flowers
that bloomed in spring, pure like spring water
that runs downstream. Her smiles radiated joy
and whoever felt the love burning inside of her
was forever blessed. She was a child who saw
the world as good, where love triumphed.
Excited to share her love with whoever needed it
most. Naive and inexperienced, she said yes to
everything asked of her, after all, she just wanted
to be kind.
"Oh, you want my watch? There, you can have
it."
She'd given it to her classmate.
"Oh, you want me to give you, my lunch. Okay
here"
She'd given it to her classmate. But so young,
one she'd known for a while, came into her
rainbow world and caused an earthquake. He
called her by her rosy name to which she
responded with tenderness.
"Would you like to play a game with me?"
He asked her, she said no.
"Come on, you'll like it, I promise,"
He said, the child had turned her kind eyes on
him.

"Okay"
She followed him to a place, a room, she knew
that room well, she'd played with her siblings
there. She loved to turn chalk into powder, add
some water, mix and call it "food" and use her
kitchen toys to "cook" for her "kids" who were
very chunky dolls. She dreamed of being a
pediatrician someday. Even as a young child she
knew the importance of children in this world
and knew they needed to be taken care of and be
protected.
He went into a corner and asked her to remain
where she was and that she couldn't peek.
Confused, she did as he said and waited for him.
He had come out in a way she wasn't familiar
with. There was something in between his legs
she didn't recognize. He called her over, and she
hesitantly came over.
"You can trust me."
He sat her on his lap, opening a door to a new
world no child should know so young. He had
left her with a flower covered in red.
Naive and inexperienced, she had said,
"I just fell and hurt myself."
To which he agreed.
He told her previously-
"It's our little secret, don't tell your mommy and
daddy, because they won't love you anymore If
they know."

She agreed. He was there, sending her smiles, winking at her, reminding her to keep quiet. What did it all mean? But if only it were the only time this had happened. Her mind was processing things, her body aching for something she couldn't comprehend. Another who she'd known very well, this one was family. They were close. She called him cousin and he called her the same. They laughed a lot together, and he teased her a lot too but that's what family does. Families love each other even though they argue all the time. But was this an act of love? He looked into her eyes and asked her to do it when all she simply wanted was the time. She wanted to know how long till mommy came home from work. If you want me to tell you what time it is you have to do it,"
He said pointing to an area she had seen before. She didn't understand what he meant but for some unknown reason, she felt obligated to get it done. So, she did. He took pleasure in her innocence, whatever was left of it. A kind-hearted child like her did not see demons, she saw angels who were just different from the rest. It took 10 years and moving away from home to understand that her world had shattered. The rain never stopped. Thunder and storms were all her world knew. Denial, denial but the rage was proof enough. She had questions.

"Why did I do it?"
"Why did I let them touch me?"
"Why couldn't I see it through?"
She was just five and what exactly does a five-year-old know in such a petite and defenseless body? Months passed with the burden buried in her soul. She spent a lot of time staring at pictures of herself when she was younger. She giggled sometimes at her sassiness through the way she posed for the pictures but she also teared up because inside she was wounded.

"It was all my fault, I did this. I am disgusting"
This was who she saw staring back at her. She hated her, she was ugly. What she would give to cut her face off, her skin off. She had cried one night and rushed to her parent's kitchen; She pulled out the biggest knife they had and held it to her arm.

"What are you doing?"
Her mother asked.
"What were you going to do with that knife?"
She knew.
"Are you trying to hurt yourself?"
She knew.
"Yes"
That night, she opened up to her mother about those who had tormented her. "Why didn't you tell me this earlier? You should've come to me".

She should've but she couldn't. She hated herself
for letting this happen to her, not once, not
twice. How could she have faced the one who
only saw beauty in her? Rotten was who she
was, faded, used and who could ever love
someone like that?
Both sharing tears, she had felt some relief, but
it wasn't over. A sudden fear of him coming to
hurt her had swallowed her, keeping her hidden
in the dark, anxious. Opening up to her mother
didn't stop the pain, especially when she didn't
believe it when she mentioned that the cousin
had done something too.
Mommy said he was ill, that he was incapable of
such an act. It got her to question if it was even
real, but it must have been, it was stuck in her
mind like a disease. The sick feeling going up
her throat. Was her body even her own
anymore? She was uncomfortable in her own
skin. The bullying she got from school about her
appearance didn't help, it made it all worse.
Lost, she found herself living her youth in
despair. Her world crumbled with every painful
passing day. Everyday felt the same, she was
stuck in a loop that only brought tears once the
lights went out. She started a habit of carving
her pain into her arm, legs, thighs, and palm.
Constant fantasies of what it would feel like to
bleed till there was nothing left but a dry, cold

corpse. Whatever happiness felt like she knew nothing of it.

Darkness invaded what was once so clear, the little sparkle she had left disappeared, and death became her only hope. Yet, she still managed to laugh sometimes while she was torn. But in that deep pit of hopelessness, she found a light. A light she was born with but was unaware of.

A God-given talent. She was a writer; her pain was the story and her blood the ink. It poured out of her like a flood. What once made her weak has given her strength to feel it all again and come out alive. It gave her purpose, she fought but hasn't lost. When she believed she'd fail, she succeeded, proving to herself she was more than her past. She was magical, building her world back up with the light she carried within. Her smiles became more genuine, her heart began to glow again, and her touches were like the divine, honest and pure.

I Met a Man

As much as it hurts to be in pain, it does feel
good,
because it's real.
The best way to know if you're still alive is to
cut through your skin and watch as blood rains
and stains your bed sheets. Then a scream
follows, one heavy with anguish, years of
suppressed emotions, loneliness, and pain.
A scream that carries tears made of fine glass.
I am not ready to be happy because it feels like
one of those things that won't last forever.
I am not ready to be loved because it feels like
one of those things that don't last forever.
I am deeply wounded and emotionally gutted.
I am not ready to smile because it feels like one
of those things that won't last forever.
Yet I met a man with kind eyes, but I searched
for high tones and disagreements.
He saw through me, so I hated him more.
He has no right to love me,
He has no right to make me feel so high,
He has no right to distract me from my painful
reality.
I met a man who held me softly, but I searched
for anger and aggression.

He has no right to make me feel…wanted,
He has no right to look at me with those eyes
that cracked my walls.
He has no right to make me laugh and show me
that the world isn't so bad.

I met a man with a stable mind,
He has no right to accept my instability,
He has no right to trust me,
He has no right to tell me It's going to be okay.
He is confusing me.
I met a man whose arms wrapped around my
waist at night,
Whose eyes only searched for mine,
Whose hands only held mine.
He has no right to love me,
He has no right to care for me.
Because I convinced myself a man like him
could never love a woman like me,
Because I convinced myself the scars on my
skin would repulse him,
I convinced myself the trauma would scare him.
But he walks with me in the morning,
Lays with me at night,
sits with me while I meditate.
I met a man who loves me,
I have no right to hate him for it.

Liberated Soul

Addiction had me question God's intentions.
I told him it was self-expression to inhale these
medications and watch erotic productions. They
sent me to another dimension. It became an
obligation to follow this rotation. Where I'm
from that routine gave me validation, who am I
to protest such glorification?
These chicks would feel me up and look at me
with admiration. I gave them what they wanted a
night of fornication where we were slaves to our
bodies' needs. The orgasmic sensation took us to
a euphoric fantasy. It "healed" this illness we
called pain.
Not long after, I depended on these remedies to
satisfy my depression. Frustration became a
daily emotion. Destruction and arson become
part of my rotation. Fatal attractions, possessive
affections, and dreadful relations overwhelmed
my life.
Addiction had me question God's intentions and
I owed him an explanation. Shame held me at
knifepoint and condemnation had me isolating
myself from him. Death was the goal, who have
I become? I was filthy.

My soul was rotten, my heart was darkened, and
my spirit poisoned.
He called me once more and asked me to come
to him. I made a confession. My spirit was dying
of dehydration and he poured himself into me.
His protective veil surrounded me, my delusions
and foolishness were replaced with wisdom. I
moved to a new rhythm.
Where I came from had a new perception of me,
I was no longer like them and was no longer
impressed by their actions. They excluded me
and chased me out. They thought they left me in
the dirt but God has washed me of my filth.
I was submerged in clean, pure water and was
born again. I learned God was not a God of
confusion but one of Salvation.

Emerging from the Darkness

Mommy said she was as beautiful as the flowers
that bloomed in spring, pure like spring water
that runs downstream. Her smiles radiated joy
and whoever felt the love burning inside of her
was forever blessed. She was a child who saw
the world as good, where love triumphed.
Excited to share her love with whoever needed it
most. Naive and inexperienced, she said yes to
everything asked of her, after all, she just wanted
to be kind.
"Oh, you want my watch? There, you can have
it."
She'd given it to her classmate.
"Oh, you want me to give you, my lunch. Okay
here"
She'd given it to her classmate. But so young,
one she'd known for a while, came into her
rainbow world and caused an earthquake. He
called her by her rosy name to which she
responded with tenderness.
"Would you like to play a game with me?"
He asked her, she said no.
"Come on, you'll like it, I promise,"
He said, the child had turned her kind eyes on
him.

"Okay"

She followed him to a place, a room, she knew
that room well, she'd played with her siblings
there. She loved to turn chalk into powder, add
some water, mix and call it "food" and use her
kitchen toys to "cook" for her "kids" who were
very chunky dolls. She dreamed of being a
pediatrician someday. Even as a young child she
knew the importance of children in this world
and knew they needed to be taken care of and be
protected.

He went into a corner and asked her to remain
where she was and that she couldn't peek.
Confused, she did as he said and waited for him.
He had come out in a way she wasn't familiar
with. There was something in between his legs
she didn't recognize. He called her over, and she
hesitantly came over.

"You can trust me."

He sat her on his lap, opening a door to a new
world no child should know so young. He had
left her with a flower covered in red.

Naive and inexperienced, she had said,

"I just fell and hurt myself."

To which he agreed.

He told her previously-

"It's our little secret, don't tell your mommy and
daddy, because they won't love you anymore If
they know."

She agreed. He was there, sending her smiles, winking at her, reminding her to keep quiet. What did it all mean? But if only it were the only time this had happened. Her mind was processing things, her body aching for something she couldn't comprehend. Another who she'd known very well, this one was family. They were close. She called him cousin and he called her the same. They laughed a lot together, and he teased her a lot too but that's what family does. Families love each other even though they argue all the time. But was this an act of love? He looked into her eyes and asked her to do it when all she simply wanted was the time. She wanted to know how long till mommy came home from work. If you want me to tell you what time it is you have to do it,"
He said pointing to an area she had seen before. She didn't understand what he meant but for some unknown reason, she felt obligated to get it done. So, she did. He took pleasure in her innocence, whatever was left of it. A kind-hearted child like her did not see demons, she saw angels who were just different from the rest. It took 10 years and moving away from home to understand that her world had shattered. The rain never stopped. Thunder and storms were all her world knew. Denial, denial but the rage was proof enough. She had questions.

"Why did I do it?"
"Why did I let them touch me?"
"Why couldn't I see it through?"
She was just five and what exactly does a five-year-old know in such a petite and defenseless body? Months passed with the burden buried in her soul. She spent a lot of time staring at pictures of herself when she was younger. She giggled sometimes at her sassiness through the way she posed for the pictures, but she also teared up because inside she was wounded.
"It was all my fault, I did this. I am disgusting"
This was who she saw staring back at her. She hated her, she was ugly. What she would give to cut her face off, her skin off. She had cried one night and rushed to her parent's kitchen; She pulled out the biggest knife they had and held it to her arm.
"What are you doing?"
Her mother asked.
"What were you going to do with that knife?"
She knew.
"Are you trying to hurt yourself?"
She knew.
"Yes"
That night, she opened up to her mother about those who had tormented her. "Why didn't you tell me this earlier? You should've come to me".

She should've but she couldn't. She hated herself
for letting this happen to her, not once, not
twice. How could she have faced the one who
only saw beauty in her? Rotten was who she
was, faded, used and who could ever love
someone like that?
Both sharing tears, she had felt some relief, but
it wasn't over. A sudden fear of him coming to
hurt her had swallowed her, keeping her hidden
in the dark, anxious. Opening up to her mother
didn't stop the pain, especially when she didn't
believe it when she mentioned that the cousin
had done something too.
Mommy said he was ill, that he was incapable of
such an act. It got her to question if it was even
real, but it must have been, it was stuck in her
mind like a disease. The sick feeling going up
her throat. Was her body even her own
anymore? She was uncomfortable in her own
skin. The bullying she got from school about her
appearance didn't help, it made it all worse.
Lost, she found herself living her youth in
despair. Her world crumbled with every painful
passing day. Everyday felt the same, she was
stuck in a loop that only brought tears once the
lights went out. She started a habit of carving
her pain into her arm, legs, thighs, and palm.
Constant fantasies of what it would feel like to
bleed till there was nothing left but a dry, cold

corpse. Whatever happiness felt like she knew nothing of it.

Darkness invaded what was once so clear, the little sparkle she had left disappeared, and death became her only hope. Yet, she still managed to laugh sometimes while she was torn. But in that deep pit of hopelessness, she found a light. A light she was born with but was unaware of.

A God-given talent. She was a writer; her pain was the story and her blood the ink. It poured out of her like a flood. What once made her weak has given her strength to feel it all again and come out alive. It gave her purpose, she fought but hasn't lost. When she believed she'd fail, she succeeded, proving to herself she was more than her past. She was magical, building her world back up with the light she carried within. Her smiles became more genuine, her heart began to glow again, and her touches were like the divine, honest and pure.

The Cries of the Beloved

I am so tired.
I wrote on the wall with blood dripping from my
arm. I sat down on the ground,
Staring at the pool of blood before me,
feeling defeated, feeling numb. Then it came out
of the shadows with a satisfied grin, Its
blood-colored eyes staring at me.

Tell me, how does it feel?

It asked while its long, veiny arms stretched to
reach my face.

Mmm, don't be so sad, in due time you'll be
free.

I was desperate to be free.
Its long nails ran across my face as it looked into
my eyes, It slowly pushed them into my skin as I
cried in agony.
Blood ran down my face and fell into my mouth;
I tasted it. When it pulled away, there was a
piece of my skin hanging from its nails.
Sweating and breathing heavily, I watched as it
ate my flesh.

Painful, it tastes painful.

It said while I held my bloody face, horrified.
I've been in this room with flickering red lights
for an unknown time. Sometimes, the light
would go out, and I'd crunch up in the corner,
anxious and alert. It came without warning,
tortured me, and promised me freedom. I never
asked how it was planning on doing that, but it
would never tell me.

Why won't it just kill me?

It knew how to get in my head and send me back
to times that shattered my heart.
I never sleep because sometimes it would choke
me. I am an ant compared to him, it could
swallow me whole in one gulp. I wanted to leave
this place, I wanted to get out of its suffocating
grip.

"Why don't you ever try to take me down?"

It growled and I was waiting for it to laugh
because it was a joke right? How could I take
this ginormous filth down? I am a bug, it can
pick me up from the ground with the tip of his

nails. There was no fighting this thing and coming out alive.
"Why are you mocking me?"
I asked.
"Admit it, you love it when I break you piece by piece. You love it when I inhale the little light you have left."
It smirked, it's smile centimeters wide,
its long and Sharp teeth tempted my fear.
I needed to get out of this hole but no doors could open; They were there to give me the illusion that I could escape but those doors would disappear when I touched the handles. My tears could fill up the ocean if it ever ran dry. The amount of blood I lost could bring the dead back to life. It smiled at every twist and turn I made out of anguish and hatred. This time I was certain it was going to kill me. It wrapped a metal chain around my neck and pulled as tight as it could so my head could detach from my body. I looked up as my last drop of tears ran down my face. As my tears fell, the ceiling opened up, and the blinding light had me looking away. I gasped as it let go of the chain causing me to fall on my knees. I could feel my soul coming back to me. The white lights brightened the room and I watched as the beast caught on fire shouting in pain…it knew my pain now.

The chains turned to ash and a door opened up,
revealing a golden path.

Be free.

The light spoke before it disappeared.
I walked down the golden path barefooted. My
stained clothes vanished and I had on a white
robe and my skin was clean. My hair fell on my
shoulders, soft and clean. My nails short and
washed.
My vision cleared and below me there were
white clouds and the vast ocean.
Above there were golden clouds and beside me
multiple golden skyscrapers.
I looked behind me and it was all gone.
Everything that happened before this moment
was turned to ash and faded away.

I was free.

You're Wrong About US!

We carry a cross the world has placed on our
shoulders
We fall to our knees, look up, Pray to our Lord
for strength,
Ask him
"How could they be so wrong about us?"
Why do we have to carry this burden when
we've done nothing to deserve this punishment?
Lord, how could they be so wrong?"
He responds
"Great Kings are persecuted because others
know the power they hold, and they fear that
power".
Everything you think about us is wrong. From
defining us based on the color of our skin, To
treating us like delinquents, push us to the
ground like bugs.
We don't beg for hugs
we deserve to be treated like human beings
Everything you think about us is wrong
From assuming we're danger when clearly it's
the power we embody you fear our light
blinding
our purpose beyond your undertsanding.

The hatred that runs through your veins for our
dark skin is non-ending and wrong.
The endless tears we've shed for freedom while
you watched and mocked is wrong
We keep our children close to our chest
Keep them safe from the world that has treated
us so unfairly
We scream out our Lord's name
with his strength, we stand and say
"Everything you think about us is wrong"
We're warriors, royalty and power.

Neglected Spirits

Easily influenced,
Constantly misled.
Provoking views and clouded judgments,
Wicked tendencies and damaged self-esteem.
Filled with pride but stained by lustful impulses
and twisted ideals.
False preaches about love,
It's all so conditional.
Trading intimacy for cash,
Battle of the sexes, who's better off without the
other?
Dividing what is meant to be Devine.
I don't need you but I'll use you to fulfill my
emptiness and whatever I desire.
When has everything become nothing?
He checked so many boxes yet I chose to send
him on his way, to then ask
"Where are the good men?"
And push a narrative
"What are men for?"
To then answer with ignorance believing that
you're better than the rest.
It is foolish to put yourself above others.
-

We're Tempted to follow their ways.

It all looks so glamorous and we become
envious.
But it's all an act, a performance to feast on our
hidden wounds,
selling temporary fixes with permanent
consequences to neglected spirits.
-

Sex appeal makes up for the lack of character
these days.
He calls you baby when his body is in need
He never calls you when your heart is in need.
You give him what he wants and you feel in
control…
But are YOU really in control?
-

Or is it these meddling voices who whisper in
your ears to dominate your mind and heart. To
manipulate your emotions, deceive your sight
and paralyze your purpose.
They know they've already sent you to your
demise.
Or is it the ones who disguise themselves as
friendly and trustworthy while they hope you
fall in the pit with them.
They play with you like a puppet while they
laugh, satisfied as you sink deeper in the
darkness….alone.